SandCastle

Word Families Set 1

-ad as in dad

Mary Elizabeth Salzmann

Consulting Editor Monica Marx, M.A./Reading Specialist

ABDO Publishing Company

Published by SandCastle™, an imprint of ABDO Publishing Company, 4940 Viking Drive, Edina, Minnesota 55435.

Printed in the United States.

Credits
Edited by: Pam Price
Curriculum Coordinator: Nancy Tuminelly
Cover and Interior Design and Production: Mighty Media
Photo Credits: Brand X Pictures, Corbis Images, Eyewire Images, Hemera, PhotoDisc, Stockbyte

Library of Congress Cataloging-in-Publication Data

Salzmann, Mary Elizabeth, 1968-
    -Ad as in dad / Mary Elizabeth Salzmann.
        p. cm. -- (Word families. Set I)
    Summary: Introduces, in brief text and illustrations, the use of the letter combination "ad" in such words as "dad," "mad," "pad," and "sad."
    ISBN 1-59197-226-4
    1. Readers (Primary) [1. Vocabulary. 2. Reading.] I. Title.

PE1119 .S234213 2003
728.1--dc21
                                                    2002038624

SandCastle™ books are created by a professional team of educators, reading specialists, and content developers around five essential components that include phonemic awareness, phonics, vocabulary, text comprehension, and fluency. All books are written, reviewed, and leveled for guided reading, early intervention reading, and Accelerated Reader® programs and designed for use in shared, guided, and independent reading and writing activities to support a balanced approach to literacy instruction.

Let Us Know

After reading the book, SandCastle would like you to tell us your stories about reading. What is your favorite page? Was there something hard that you needed help with? Share the ups and downs of learning to read. We want to hear from you! To get posted on the ABDO Publishing Company Web site, send us e-mail at:

sandcastle@abdopub.com

SandCastle Level: Transitional

-ad Words

dad

glad

lad

mad

pad

sad

Val colors with her dad.

Swinging makes Tory glad.

Good grades mean
Jon is a smart lad.

Pat hammers when he is mad.

Tim writes on a pad.

Ally's mom holds her
when she feels sad.

Brad and His Dad

Brad and his dad
went fishing at Lake Chad.

They fished all day,

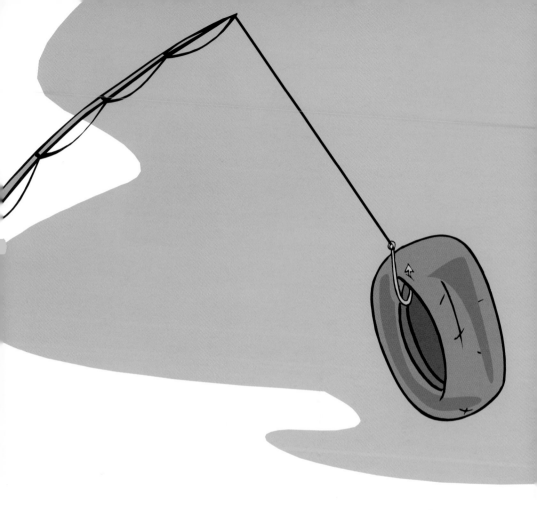

but there were no fish
to be had.

"It's a nice sunny day.
Let's go for a hike,"
said Brad's dad.

So they began to hike
around Lake Chad.

Brad and his dad
saw a frog.

It was sitting
on a lily pad.

Brad and his dad
heard a loon call.

They couldn't tell if the
sound was happy or sad.

They saw two cute, furry
rabbits and the sight
made Brad glad.

In the end,
the trip wasn't bad.

In fact, Brad thought
it was totally rad!

The -ad Word Family

bad	had
Brad	lad
Chad	mad
clad	pad
dad	rad
fad	sad
glad	tad

Glossary

Some of the words in this list may have more than one meaning. The meaning listed here reflects the way the word is used in the book.

hike   to take a long walk, especially in the country

lily pad   the floating leaf of a water lily

loon   a water bird that lives near lakes and can dive and swim under water

rad   short form of the word radical that is slang for great or terrific

squirrel   a rodent that has a bushy tail and lives in trees

About SandCastle™

A professional team of educators, reading specialists, and content developers created the SandCastle™ series to support young readers as they develop reading skills and strategies and increase their general knowledge. The SandCastle™ series has four levels that correspond to early literacy development in young children. The levels are provided to help teachers and parents select the appropriate books for young readers.

Emerging Readers
(no flags)

Beginning Readers
(1 flag)

Transitional Readers
(2 flags)

Fluent Readers
(3 flags)

These levels are meant only as a guide. All levels are subject to change.

To see a complete list of SandCastle™ books and other nonfiction titles from ABDO Publishing Company, visit **www.abdopub.com** or contact us at:

4940 Viking Drive, Edina, Minnesota 55435 • 1-800-800-1312 • fax: 1-952-831-1632